This book belongs to

....

D1643593

make
believe
ideas

Sleeping Beauty

Key sound long ee spellings: ea, ee, ie
Secondary sounds: ea, ou, long oo

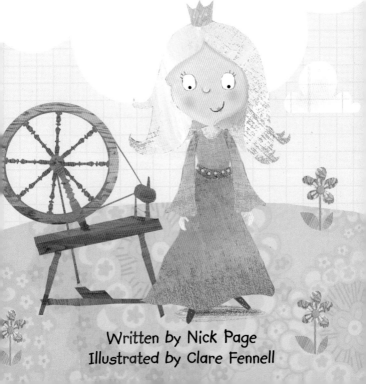

Written by Nick Page
Illustrated by Clare Fennell

Reading with phonics

How to use this book

The **Reading with phonics** series helps you to have fun with your child and to support their learning of phonics and reading. It is aimed at children who have learned the letter sounds and are building confidence in their reading.

Each title in the series focuses on a different key sound. The entertaining retelling of the story repeats this sound frequently, and the different spellings for the sound are highlighted in red type. The first activity at the back of the book provides practice in reading and using words that contain this sound. The key sound for **Sleeping Beauty** is the long ee.

Start by reading the story to your child, asking them to join in with the refrain in bold. Next, encourage them to read the story with you. Give them a hand to decode tricky words.

Now look at the activity pages at the back of the book. These are intended for you and your child to enjoy together. Most are not activities to complete in pencil or pen, but by reading and talking or pointing.

The **Key sound** pages focus on one sound, and on the various different groups of letters that produce that sound. Encourage your child to read the different letter groups and complete the activity, so they become more aware of the variety of spellings there are for the same sound.

The **Letters together** pages look at three pairs or groups of letters and at the sounds they make as they work together. Help your child to read the words and trace the route on the word maps.

Rhyme is used a lot in these retellings. Whatever stage your child has reached in their learning of phonics, it is always good practice for them to listen carefully for sounds and find words that rhyme. The pages on **Rhyming words** take six words from the story and ask children to read and find other words that rhyme with them.

The **Key words** pages focus on a number of key words that occur regularly but can nonetheless be tricky. Many of these words are not sounded out following the rules of phonics and the easiest thing is for children to learn them by sight, so that they do not worry about decoding them. These pages encourage children to retell the story, practising key words as they do so.

The **Picture dictionary** page asks children to focus closely on nine words from the story. Encourage children to look carefully at each word, cover it with their hand, write it on a separate piece of paper, and finally, check it!

Do not complete all the activities at once – doing one each time you read will ensure that your child continues to enjoy the stories and the time you are spending together. **Have fun!**

Once a happy king and queen
held a feast upon the green
to meet and greet their baby girl,
whose name was Celestine.

Spinning wheel, spin for me,
seven fairies came to tea!

The fairies bowed before the queen.
The smallest one (called Geraldine) said,
"Thank you for inviting us,
we've gifts for Celestine!"

Spinning wheel, spin for me,
they gave six blessings cheerfully.

But then, along came Greasy Jean,
a nasty fairy, bad and mean.
She hadn't been invited, so
she cursed young Celestine.

"Spinning wheel, spin for me,
touch the needle, dead she'll be!"

Geraldine said, "Calm your fears.
I've one more gift, as it appears.
No one will die, but everyone
will sleep for years and years."

"Spinning wheel, spin for me,
love's first kiss shall be the key!"

As she grew, her mum, the queen,
warned her darling Celestine,
'Don't ever touch a spindle, for
you don't know where it's been."

Spinning wheel, spin for me,
you'll be safe, I guarantee!

When the princess reached sixteen,
she found a room she'd never seen,
and in it was a spinning wheel.
She touched and gave a scream!

Spinning wheel,
spin for me,
the spell has worked,
as you will see!

You could hardly hear a peep:
all the servants, dreaming deep,
king and queen and Celestine –
all of them – asleep.

Spinning wheel, spin for me,
now that's what I call sorcery!

17

They sleep for many, many years.
The castle almost disappears
beneath the creeping ivy, till,
one day, a prince appears.

Spinning wheel, spin for me,
he cuts his way through bush and tree!

Inside, the prince finds Celestine,
the sweetest girl he's ever seen.
He kisses her, which wakes them all –
the servants, king, and queen.

Spinning wheel, spin for me,
true love's kiss has set her free!

Very soon, the king and queen
hold one more feast upon the green
to celebrate the wedding of
the prince and Celestine!

Spinning wheel, spin for me,
a happy ending, oh, yippee!

23

Key sound

There are several different groups of letters that make the **long ee** sound. Practise them by making some blessings for Celestine. First use each word in a different blessing.

belief

niece

brief

piece

field

movie

please

teach

each

clean

reach

eat

see

een

sixteen

sleep

en

keep

Now try using two or three of the fairies' words in the same blessing!

Letters together

Look at these pairs of letters and say
the sounds they make.

ea   **ou**   **oo**

Follow the words that contain **ea** to
find the queen's tears.

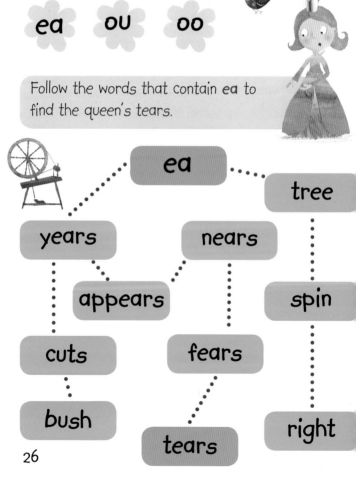

ea

tree

years   nears

appears   spin

cuts   fears

bush   right

tears

26

Follow the words that contain **ou** to lead the prince to the house.

ou ···· green

found

our ···· ground

about ····· mouse · mean

sound ···· house · wheel

Follow the words that contain the **long oo** to show this fairy the way to the moon!

oo · boot

free · room

· spoon

soon

inside ··· very · moon

Rhyming words

Read the words in the flowers and point to other words that rhyme with them.

bakes	**wakes**	girl
wheel		cakes

keep	**sleep**	deep
baby		fairy

fears	**years**	bush
appears		king

sleep	nasty
sea	pea

tea

gift	well
green	fell

spell

needle	ivy
miss	hiss

kiss

Now choose a word and make up a rhyming chant!

Greasy Jean has **been seen** on the **green**!

Key words

Many common words can be tricky to sound out. Practise them by reading these sentences from the story. Now make more sentences using other key words from around the border.

Seven fairies **gave** the baby gifts.

Geraldine made **another** spell so Celestine would sleep.

Everyone in the palace fell asleep.

Greasy Jean cast **a** spell.

things • her • of • another

a • everyone • after • wanted • eat • our • to • has • ye

The prince and princess **got** married!

The prince pushed **through** tall bushes.

Greasy Jean was not invited **to** the party.

The king and queen **gave** a party for their baby.

Celestine hurt **her** finger on a spinning wheel.

They slept for a **long** time.

got • other • through • never • long • took • again • would • gave • well • must

ught • more • magic • find • round • tree • shouted •

Picture dictionary

Look carefully at the pictures and the words.
Now cover the words, one at a time.
Can you remember how to write them?

baby

fairy

gifts

ivy

king

prince

princess

queen

spinning
wheel